WORLD'S GREATEST GOLF EXCUSES

**All the GOOD Reasons —
for Playing so BAD in the 1990's**

by

Hal Gevertz & Mark Oman

Illustrations by D. Goodwin

A Golfaholics Anonymous Book

Published by Golfaholics Anonymous®
P.O. Box 222357
Carmel, CA 93922

Library of Congress Catalog Number: 89-081851
International Standard Book Number: 0917346-03-3

Printed in the United States of America

*"Like a conch shell at the beach,
if you pick up a golfer and hold him close to your ear
— you will hear an alibi."*

Fred Beck

CONTENTS

"Whadaya mean? It was a gimmie!"

THE IMPORTANCE
OF THE
GREAT EXCUSE

Anyone who has ever taken club in hand with intent to commit a felony on an insignificant pock-marked little ball knows there are a thousand reasons for playing like a putz — or a putzette, as the case may be.

Until now, the problem has been in separating all the good, righteous, legitimate alibis from the unbelievably dumb excuses some golfers try to get away with.

The fact is that in this day of space age shafts, multiple wedge systems and high-tech metal woods, yesterday's hackneyed, tired old alibis such as: *I was attacked by a mob of killer gnats in the parking lot,* just don't cut it anymore.

Because, let's face it folks, even with all the state-of-the-art equipment, 14 clubs still isn't enough the way most of us play the game. Our only hope to save the day and salvage what's left of our ravaged self-esteem is to have a whole bagful of great excuses ready to aim and fire!

Besides, when you're spending big bucks to play great golf courses, you simply can't afford to be caught with anything less than a 24K excuse to explain the pain and suffering you've just paid dearly to put yourself through.

If we are ever to reach the heights of the PGA and LPGA Pros we idealize on television, we can't be satisfied with third rate, bourgeois alibis.

The great players don't rely on tired old excuses to explain an off round. The mark of a true champion is the ability to dazzle the opposition with an arsenal of mindboggling, inspirational alibis that give a whole new dimension to the phrase, *improving one's lie.*

And since we've broached the subject of *lies,* it is shocking to note that while the Rules of Golf takes great pains to distinguish between a *playable lie* and an *unplayable lie,* no one has made the least effort to do the same for golf excuses.

Until now! This book is an attempt to rectify this appalling oversight in hopes that the world's golfers will never forget what all the great players have known since the game began: When you are able to stop another golfer in his tracks — or better yet, in his backswing — with a great excuse he actually has to think about, you are taking his mind off his own game, and perhaps even causing him to worry about the excuse he is going to need for the shot *he* is about to throw away.

With that in mind, and after thousands of hours of painstaking research, we have concluded that all the great and highly *playable* golf excuses fall into three Primary Excuse Species:

1. Equipment
2. Other People
3. Natural Forces

We will examine these three species, as well as some International Excuses, so you can alibi like the natives when traveling to foreign lands.

Indeed, it is not easy being humiliated and tormented week after week, year after year. As we approach the turn of the century the world golfers are going to need all the great excuses we can get.

Excuses that haven't been used and abused on every course for the last five hundred years!

Excuses you can live with.

Excuses you can stand up and be proud to proclaim.

Excuses your fellow golfers may even believe!

After all, isn't that what the game is all about?

Of course it is! For no matter how the game beats us down, as long as there's one good excuse left in our bodies, we'll be back for one more round.

"Doglegs always give me trouble..."

How you can help keep the tradition alive

The tradition of golf excuses has been going on since the very first banana ball took flight.

But only you can keep it alive. At the end of each section in this book, we have left space for you to write in your own great excuses.

By writing them down, you not only become part of golf's great heritage, but the very act of articulating them on paper adds credibility and legitimacy to your best excuses.

Writing down your tried and true excuses is also healthy and cleansing for one's mind and soul. In fact, there may be nothing better for one's handicap than a complete catharsis of all the people and things responsible for your underwhelming accomplishments on the course.

As Jay Cronley said way back in 1981:

> *As of this writing, there are approximately 2,450 reasons why a person hits a rotten shot and more are being discovered every day.*

Help us discover and record the best of these alibis. In the end you'll be able to tell your children you did your part in keeping the glorious tradition of great golf excuses alive!

"You can never have enough equipment — or enough great excuses!"

PART I

EQUIPMENT

In this section we will set forth the really good excuses relating to our golf equipment.

Obviously there are all kinds of *equipment* responsible for one's underwhelming achievements on the golf course. We have divided them into three categories:

- Hardware, Software & Underwear
- Physical Equipment
- Psychological Equipment

The great thing about blaming your equipment is that it can't defend itself. Yes, I suppose that does make it an easy out — which is exactly why it's such a great place to start!

1

Hardware, Software, & Underwear

Clubs, Bags, and Balls

"Of course I played like a yutz..."

- My clubs are too heavy.
- My clubs are too light.
- My clubs are old and dirty.
- My clubs are brand new and I didn't want to get them dirty.

Sound familiar? Well, I'm sorry troops, but you just can't get away with hackneyed old alibis like that anymore. It's just not good enough to plead:

- My grips are too slippery.

Even if they are, do you really expect anybody to believe you? This is the 1990's. You're going to have to be more creative and dynamic than that.

In this high-tech world of beryilium copper irons and carbon woods, you have to be just as high-tech in your alibis...

- These clubs are the worst. How can you swing anything that doesn't have the feel of forged carbon steel, the forgiveness of cavity-back perimeter weighting and still have the good looks of a blade?

You see how by using specifics and being authoritative, you create credibility. Think of it as the *verisimilitude factor*.

On second thought...

"My grips are too slippery."

Think you've got the idea, now? Then let's tee it up and go for it!

"My long game's miserable, but..."

- I just spent a fortune having these woods refinished. I hit it like that on purpose so I won't scratch the clubface.

- I haven't had time to chisel the asphalt out of the grooves of my 7-wood.

- The spike marks on top of the head of my classic 1960 Eye-O-Matic MacGregor Tourney Driver make me hyperventilate.

- The grip on my driver is losing some of its traction action right where the last three fingers on my left hand need to hang on so I don't lose it past parallel and have to release prematurely...

- It's been so bad I went back to my old Tommy Bolt woods. Slice the hell out of 'em, but that driver sure throws great!

"I know my putting stinks..."

- But my kid took my favorite putter to the miniature golf course and threw it down the wishing well!

- But it *pings* so loud it gives me a headache!

- I even tried one of those long handled putters. Got it all lined up — then jammed the grip up my nose.

- My pro says I have severe *focal dystonia syndrome* and for the next six weeks anything inside the flagstick is a gimmie... I swear!

"I never blame my clubs — it's my shafts!"

- If God had wanted us to play with metal shafts, He would have given us titanium trees!

- My shafts are much too stiff. You'd have to be Hogan to swing these things — Hulk Hogan!

- My shafts are too whippy. Think I need a tad more boron to strengthen the tip and isolate my flex point. On the other hand, maybe my high modulus fibers are too modulus...

Now, at least, you sound like a pro. (Don't worry, nobody else will have any idea what you're talking about either.)

"Think I need a tad more boron to isolate my flex point."

"I know I played like a dufus, but..."

■ My bag is so old and ugly it makes me swing old and ugly.

■ My bag is so big I have to carry more stuff than I ever will need; which means even more decisions about which glove, what color ball, what length tees, coin or plastic logo ball-marker, visor or cap, sunscreen with a 15 SPF or a 26 SPF. Then after I decide and finally find what I'm looking for, I've also found an old scorecard from the last time I played this course and one look at it and I'd just as soon spend the day catching up on some free root-canal work — a Christmas present from my mother-in-law who bowls five nights a week... when she's not doing one-nighters on the senior mud-wrestling circuit.

■ It's tough to keep that killer instinct for 18 holes when you've got Mickey Mouse and Goofy plastered all over your bag.

■ I just can't get used to these new fangled full-length, fleece-lined dividers. They just don't give me the confidence my old four-compartment fur-lined dividers did.

"A basketball is a basketball, but a golf ball is a spinning sphere with a turbulent, viscose boundary layer."

■ That's easy for you to say, but to me it will always be an impelled non-oblatious alveolate spheroid.

■ My balls are too old. They just don't go like they used to. And neither do I.

■ With these new hot balls I can air mail it anytime I want. I just don't always put the right zip code on it.

■ High trajectory... Low Trajectory... Orange... Yellow... Two-tone... 90 Compression... 100 Compression... Balata... Surlyn... One-piece ball... Two-piece ball... Balls with dimples... Balls with pimples... Liquid center... Wound core... Soft feel for putting... Hard and fast off the clubhead... Greater distance... More accuracy... Low spin rolls forever... High spin sucks like a leech...

I'm telling you, they just don't make the right ball for the shot I had!

■ A friend of mine just tried some lithium-covered balls. Isn't lithium the stuff they use to cheer up manic-depressives? No wonder it's on golf balls!

When all else fails, <u>always</u> blame the ball. Everybody knows that with 9,369,274 combinations of ball types to choose from, you will never ever have just the right ball for the shot you have to play. Which is why your best excuse when it comes to balls is:

■ Not my fault. All the pro shop had was icosahedral and octahedral dimple balls and there's no way you can play this course with anything but dodecahedron balls.

Now who's going to argue with that?

Of course, there is one exception to the above. The hole-in-one. This is one shot where the specific type of ball is irrelevant since the greatness of the shot was obviously due to your complete and total mastery of the mental and physical aspects of the game!

(An excuse which will probably get you more flak than all the others. But well worth it!)

Clothing

"Of course I hit it in the boonies..."

- My shoelaces came undone and tied themselves in a knot on my backswing.

- My waterproof shoes are supposed to let air in and keep water out. Instead, they let the water in and a couple of toes out!

- I scuffed my new handmade white leather shoes on the first hole and wasn't able to get any polish on them until the back nine. God it was awful!

- No way can you make that shot unless your shoes have butyl-impregnated outersoles, flex grooves in the mid-sole, and anatomically correct ceramic cleats.

"I know clothes make the golfer, but..."

■ The geometric design of my shirt didn't agree with the plaid in my pants and every time I looked down to address my shot, I got vertigo.

■ My zipper broke when I came out of the port-a-potty, and the only velcro I had was on the back of my golf glove... Don't ask.

■ My glove is full of holes and stiff as an old sweatsock.

■ My glove is all out of shape since my wife borrowed it for batting practice.

■ The only way you can sneak up on this course is to dress in combat fatigues. You think the pro shop has any pants in camouflage plaid?

■ I'd like to see you stay cool and steady on a downhill 3-footer with a 6-foot break when the wool longjohns you borrowed from your kid start itching because it's 60 degrees hotter than when you teed off!

■ The way I was dressed everybody thought I was a pro! Why do I have to tee off and spoil everything?

*"My zipper broke and the only velcroe I had was
on the back of... Don't ask."*

Golf Carts

"How can I
play good when..."

■ The cart moved slower than I can walk. Everybody knows it's the guys in the fast carts that get all the good lies.

■ The cart paths were all down the left side, and I was fading the ball all day and you can't drive across the fairways, so I never had the right club and wasn't about to hold up play by walking all the way back to get another club and would have worn myself out by the fourth hole if I had!

■ My ball was on the damn cart path all day. Why didn't they put the path on the other side where all the duffers hit it?

■ Carts are mandatory, and I only play good when I walk and carry my bag.

■ I play even better when I walk and <u>someone else</u> carries my bag!

■ I really just play for the exercise.

"I really just play for the exercise."

Magazines, Books, Videos

■ Just as I figured out the *72 Ways To Get It Close From 36 Yards* featured in one magazine, the other magazine comes out with *36 Scoring Secrets From 72 yards by 18 of the top 54 Money Winners*. Good grief!

■ That book is scarier than *Psycho* — the laws of physics for the first 12 inches of the backswing is enough to give you nightmares!

■ Just finished reading *Golf In The Kingdom*... No wonder I can't play this game!

■ My golf magazines all arrived in last night's mail. Give me a couple of weeks and I'll be fine.

■ I know I'm late, but I put on this new video last night and tried to get in the same position Fred Couples was in... You wouldn't believe how hard it was sneaking out of the hospital this morning!

"My golf magazines all arrived in last night's mail..."

PHYSICAL EQUIPMENT

Body Flaws & Needs

"I never played so awful, but then..."

- My doctor told me not to swing so hard the first couple of days after open heart surgery.

- I've never had such agony from a hangnail.

- I just got new glasses and haven't quite adjusted to the prescription.

- I have a bad back, my eyes aren't what they used to be, my legs have lost it, my nerves are shot, my stomach can't take that kind of food anymore, even my hair hurts... God, it's a bitch turning 30.

- I don't smoke, don't drink, don't fool around. No wonder I can't play worth a damn!

"Haven't quite adjusted to my new glasses..."

"I know I didn't play my usual game today, but..."

■ I think I did something to my hand when I punched out the practice range ball machine for eating all my quarters and running out of balls.

■ The damn ball machine got stuck, and I had to keep filling up buckets or let the balls go all over the place, and my husband says I never practice enough anyway, so I hit all six buckets of balls and my hands looked like a couple of fresh salmon filets from Flaherty's Fish Boutique.

■ The women's restroom on the back nine was out of order... and all the suitable trees in the rough were taken!

"Damn ball machine got stuck. My husband says
I never practice enough anyway, so..."

"All right, I played like a real scuzzball, but..."

■ If you don't lift your head up, how in hell can you see where the ball goes?

■ My teeth throb and I should be at the dentist.

■ I just came from the dentist — the guy's a 36-handicap when it comes to the novocaine shot.

■ I ate a Polish sausage and it gave me gas.

■ The snack shop ran out of Polish, and I ran out of gas!

■ I really have just one problem: I stand too close to the ball — after I've hit it.

"I know I'm off my stick, but..."

- I had too much sex last night and I'm wiped out.

- I had too much sex this morning and I'm wasted.

- I'm having anxiety attacks worrying whether too much sex is why my putts are coming up short.

- I didn't have sex this morning and I'm tense.

- I haven't had sex all week and I'm really tense.

- My wife and I haven't had sex in six months — but our Miniature Schnauzer is making up for both of us!

- My wife just made an appointment for both the dog and me to have vasectomies at the S.P.C.A.

3

PSYCHOLOGICAL EQUIPMENT

Whoever said, *the mind is a terrible thing to waste,* was not a golfer.

As noted so wisely in *The 9 Commandments of Golf,* by no one less than The Pro Upstairs (God's personal golf pro!): *To play your best golf, it helps to be out of your mind.*

When it comes to golf, nearly all of us think too much and try too hard.

Or as Walter Hagen simply put it: *Give me a man with big hands, big feet and no brains, and I will make a golfer out of him.*

Simply, you don't have to be a genius to play this game. On the other hand, on some of these new courses it couldn't hurt.

"You don't have to be a genius to play this game. On the other hand..."

"How am I supposed to keep my mind on the game when..."

- My parents are trying to lay this big guilt trip on me for playing golf instead of hanging around their 50th wedding anniversary party at some ex-politician's ranch near Santa Barbara.

- My parents didn't mind at all that I was on the course instead of hanging around their 50th wedding anniversary at some ex-politician's ranch near Santa Barbara. Maybe they don't love me??

- I broke my favorite tee on the first hole, lost my Ben Crenshaw ball-marker on the third and that damned black cat ate my lucky Great White Shark headcover on nine. Thank God I'm not superstitious!

- I just found out my wife is having an affair with my analyst — who swears he's a 17, but always seems to score...

"That's what happens when..."

- Last week my radio talk show therapist tried to neuter her station's sports director with a chainsaw — and she's the one who told me I needed a stiffer shaft!

- You take your own advice. I'm a 26 handicap — what do I know?

- You give yourself some good advice — but then you figure that no one else listens to you so why should you?

- You get stuck with a shoe salesman working in the golf department and he sold me the wrong equipment and the condition of the course was miserable and the weather was the pits for golf (should've been at the beach), and to top it off, for the last two weeks my Scorpio has been in retrograde!

- Sorry, but I've got to withdraw from the tournament unless I can blow dry my hair. I don't play anywhere unless I can blow dry my hair!*

Well, that's what Ben Crenshaw said, and he got away with it!

Yes, the longer you play this game the more it becomes absolutely clear that nearly all the reasons we golf so miserably have nothing to do with us!

Never mind that today's *new age* gurus believe *what goes around, comes around*. They obviously know nothing about golf where *what goes around* usually doesn't go in the hole!

So, if it isn't our equipment that double-crosses us, and we're certainly not about to fall for this self-improvement *personal responsibility* mumbo-jumbo, then it can only be Other People who are to blame.

If you don't believe that, turn the page.*

But first, now it's your turn! Add your greatest golf excuses on the facing page.

YOUR GREATEST GOLF EXCUSES

Equipment-related alibis:

- _____
  _____
- _____
  _____
- _____
  _____
- _____
  _____
- _____
  _____
- _____
  _____
- _____
  _____
- _____
  _____
- _____
  _____
- _____
  _____

*"They were snapping pictures in the middle of my backswing —
I don't care if it was my daughter's wedding!"*

PART II

OTHER PEOPLE

Now we get to the heart and soul of great golf excuses. But first, a test.

True or false: The game is tough enough without ever accepting personal responsibility for the awful things that happen to us on the course.

TRUE, TRUE, TRUE!!

You'll notice I said *happen to us* and not *we get ourselves into.*

Never, ever blame yourself for anything that happens. No matter what, you need to feel good about yourself so you'll have the courage to continue against all odds.

When it comes to assigning serious blame for your underwhelming performance, blaming other people should be your highest priority. Attacking another person's behavior, personailty, or philosophy deflects the shame of guilt away from you and immediately puts someone else on the defensive.

Now there are three primary categories of people who deserve the brunt of blame:

1. *Spouses, Children & Animals*
2. *Golf Partners, Opponents, Caddies, the Opposite Sex & Lady Luck.*
3. *The Pros*

1

SPOUSES,
CHILDREN
& ANIMALS

Your first line of serious blame should always go right to a wife, husband, or child who is not there to defend her or himself. Besides, while the rest of your foursome may not believe your excuse, they are sure to have relatives they'd like to blame, and so probably won't argue the point.

Spouses

"That was the worst
I've ever played, but..."

- My wife/husband just doesn't understand why it's important to my emotional well-being to spend six hours chasing after a silly little ball that won't listen to anything I say and does what it DAMN WELL PLEASES JUST LIKE OUR DAUGHTER, THE DOG AND EVERYBODY ELSE IN MY LIFE!!

- My wife/husband usually gives me a bad time before I leave for the course, but this time she/he was really understanding and told me to play well, have fun and take as long as I wanted... I don't know what she/he is up to, but I don't like it!!

- My husband's planned something special for our anniversary tonight, so I rushed every shot.

- My wife's planned something special for our anniversary tonight. Hope I didn't slow you guys up too much.

- How can I keep my mind on the game. After 20 years my husband says now <u>he's ready</u> to have children!

"Please, I know what I shot, but..."

- I haven't had a chance to practice since I got out of jail for missing my last nine alimony payments.

- I just got back from my honeymoon and I'm all golfed out.

- My husband was having this tricky operation, and I wanted to get to the hospital as soon as I could, so I had to play through three foursomes on the back nine. You know how hard it is to hit it good when you play through people.

- I know my wife is having our first baby, but it took me ten months to get this starting time!

Children

"No wonder I couldn't hit the ball worth a damn..."

- Gave my kid a lesson last week and screwed up my whole swing.

- My kid gave me a lesson and screwed up my whole swing.

- My husband gave me a lesson, screwed up my whole swing, his swing, our son's swing, and his regular foursome won't return his calls!

- This dancer I met in San Francisco gave me a lesson and who the hell cares about my golf swing!

- They were snapping pictures in the middle of my backswing. I don't care if it was my daughter's wedding. She's young — there'll be another.

- I never had a chance to play as a kid. My mother was married so many times that on Father's Day I had to leave town!

Animals

When it comes to excuses dealing with the animal kingdom, most of them can probably be summed up as follows:

■ *Fish gotta swim and birds gotta fly...* But not while I'm standing over a 2-foot putt to win the match!

Here are a few more worth considering in an emergency.

■ It's bad enough when the damn gophers snatch your ball in the fairway, but when you lose your ball to the fuzzy face covering your 4-wood, it's war!

■ The water hazards were stocked with Colorado squawfish, bonytail chub and razorback sucker. You gotta be Jacques Cousteau to have a shot!

"You'd take an unplayable lie too, if..."

■ You birdied the first hole, eagled number two, and then aced Bambi on three!

■ Your ball had just been made passionate love to by a herd of over-sexed turtles, two geese-a-mating, and a 200 pound St. Bernard in heat.

"... eagled number two and then aced Bambi on three!"

2
GOLF PARTNERS, OPPONENTS, CADDIES, THE OPPOSITE SEX AND LADY LUCK

When possible, don't hesitate to lay blame on another golfer — before he does it to you.

But first let's take a second to discuss the thing that everybody on the course is guilty of — except you. Slow play.

■ It was so slow I finished reading the Sunday edition of the New York Times by the 5th hole. And I was moving my lips.

"I have nothing against using retired military for course rangers, but..."

■ When they said it was going to be a shotgun format, they weren't kidding!

■ You ever try to plumb bob a putt with an ex-Marine standing behind you with a stopwatch in one hand and a bayonet in the other?

■ They gave speeding tickets for playing too fast! Complete a round in less than five hours and they never let you play Bernhard Langer's favorite course again.

50

Partners

"It wasn't my fault we lost the match, my partner..."

■ Never gave me a chance to win a hole all day. Then on 18 he says, *I carried you all day. It's up to you...*

■ Kept telling jokes. You know how tough it is to make a 3-foot putt when you're giggling.

■ Said he was an inconsistent 12-handicap. And he was telling the truth!

■ Actually believed me when I told him I used to be a 2-handicap. Get serious!

■ You guys don't play fair — I get more strokes from my wife!

■ My partner was a member of the Audubon Society and forgot his putter. But he brought binoculars for both of us. How thoughtful!

"How do you expect me to play with confidence when..."

■ My partner runs out into the middle of the fairway as I'm teeing off. I don't care if it is the safest place to stand!

■ My partner gave me bad advice on every shot! But it sure sounded good at the time.

■ Kept rushing me. Not my fault we're three holes behind — I'm 4-putting as fast as I can!

■ My partner told me I was choking a bit earlier than usual. Hell, I was still on the driving range!

"I'm 4-putting as fast as I can!"

Opponents

"I never had a chance, my dork opponent..."

- Was a bigger sandbagger than even I am!

- Always found my ball in the rough before I did — looked like he stomped on it.

- Got real uptight just because my 5-iron missed his head by a couple of inches. Lighten up!

- Took 39 practice swings, 16 waggles and at least four or five forward presses which gave me the hebee jeebees — then kept telling me to hurry up since I was going to miss it anyway after watching him.

- Really knows how to psych me out — but then he is my shrink so...

- Smoked one cigar after another, had a bottle of booze in every compartment of his bag, had pounds of gold jewelry jangling around his neck, and a blonde playmate as his caddie... What a player!

- When you're used to everybody talking on your backswing, how can you hit a ball with all that silence? Give me a break, fellas. Yak it up!

"He really knows how to psych me out — but then he is my shrink, so..."

Caddies

The very presence of a caddie at the scene of the crime makes him an accessory. Caddies know this and understand it better than you do. Do not disappoint your caddy. Give him hell! (And a big tip.)

"I would've shot lights out if it wasn't for my caddie who..."

- Kept telling me there wasn't anything in my bag quite right for the shot I had.

- Said my new pro bag was too heavy and put my clubs in an old Sunday bag from the caddy shack. Hell, the only reason I bought the back-breaker was so a caddie could carry it!

- Said he'd been there for 30 years, yet had no idea what club I needed.

- Knew every blade of grass on the fairways, where all the hazards were, knew every hidden break in the greens, but <u>didn't know</u> a word of English.

"My caddie said he'd been there for 30 years. Who knew?"

"Some caddie..."

■ Sure I asked him what iron to use, but I also told him before we teed off not to listen to anything I said when we got out there!

■ Yeah, I lost three balls on one hole — but I kept waving the fore-caddie to move back or close his big mouth!

■ I always get the oldest cart or the youngest caddie — and neither works!

■ The guy was so frail and slow I felt sorry for him and carried the bag myself the last four holes.

■ Was so young and agile he made me feel like an old man, so I showed him how fit I really was and carried the bag myself the last four holes!

■ I asked him to read my second putt and he tells me to play for the fat part of the green!

"I always get the oldest cart or youngest caddie — and neither works!"

The Opposite Sex

"How can you concentrate on golf when..."

■ They pair you with a young lady wearing a halter top, sprayed-on jeans, and she looks like a scratch player.

■ They stick you with a threesome of men who act like *men* — particularly when you outdrive them on the first hole.

■ You try to help a man find his ball in the trees... then discover what he's looking for is a tree!

■ It's 110 degrees out there and after four holes this stud in your foursome looks like the floor show at Chippendale's.

■ The gal you're playing with looks like Dolly Parton, then tries to let it all hang out like *Big Mama* — and she does!

■ You get to the first tee and discover you're playing with Patti, Maxine and LaVerne — and they're men!

*"Tough to concentrate when you're playing with
the floor show at Chippendales."*

Lady Luck

"When it comes to playing for money..."

- I admit it. I get so nervous playing for a couple of bucks, the greens don't need fertilizing for six months!

- I don't play worth bubkas unless there's some major action. How 'bout your new Porsche for my classic '64 VW?

- The game is just no fun when you get hustled by some big time high roller.

"No fun when you get hustled by some big time high roller."

3

THE PROS

If you can't beat them, at least they're always good for an excuse. And who can blame you for trying to emulate the very best — which is precisely why they are so ripe to hang your troubles on.

And if you're playing away from your local course, don't hesitate to lay all your troubles on the hardworking shoulders of your home pro. They'll understand and forgive you. Trust me.

"My pro back home screwed up my whole right side!"

"I tried to…"

- Hitch my pants like Arnie, and gave myself a hernia.
- Smile like Seve, but my jaw got stuck.
- Joke like Trevino, but nobody laughed.
- Dress like Payne Stewart, and everybody laughed.
- Grimace and scowl like Strange, and made myself laugh.

- Toss my putter like Green, and my caddie threw it back — hard!

- Take it back slow like Lopez, and should be ready to start my downswing any day now.

- Swing like Miller Barber, and will be out of traction real soon.

- Use one of those long handle jobs like Orville Moody, but putted like Orville Redenbacher.

- Grind it out like Floyd, and cracked three gold fillings. Thanks a lot, Raymond!

■ Be swashbuckling like Chi Chi, and double-bogeyed my buckle.

■ Concentrate and be in another zone like the Golden Bear, and don't remember a thing.

■ Model my backswing after Jan Stephenson, and got asked to do a centerfold for Recreational Vehicle Quarterly.

■ Hit it with my ass like Norman, and am now singing with the Vienna Boys Choir. (Just call me the Great White Guppie!)

YOUR GREATEST EXCUSES

Alibi's you can hang on other people:

- _____
  _____
  _____
- _____
  _____
  _____
- _____
  _____
  _____
- _____
  _____
  _____
- _____
  _____
  _____
- _____
  _____
  _____
- _____
  _____
  _____
- _____
  _____
  _____
- _____
  _____
  _____
- _____
  _____

"You can't afford to let one hole screw up the entire round."

PART III

NATURAL FORCES

The following may be the best excuses of all because we truly have no control over them. When it comes to nature, you can't do much about it except blame it! Give it your best shot and we guarantee you won't get an argument back — at least not in this life!

For our purposes we'll divide Natural Forces into two sub-species:

1. Geographical
2. Meteorological

Perhaps Tom Watson said it best: *I love rotten weather. The founders of the game accepted nature for what it gave, or what it took away...*

Yes, the secret for surviving all that Mother Nature can heap upon our backswings is to not dwell in the past, but always look ahead to the future with confidence and good cheer!

For no matter what happens, you just can't afford to let one hole ruin the entire round.

1

GEOGRAPHICAL

Even the very best pros will tell you it's always the fault of the golf course.

"You call this a golf course?"

■ Look at this green — looks like the rough at the U.S. Open!

■ Look at this fairway — looks like the greens at the U.S. Open. Where's the grass?!

■ Would be nice if they moved the cup once a month — looks like they buried the greenskeeper there along with his triplex mower.

■ Fairways are so tight, it's enough to make a bowler's butt pucker.

■ The ball just doesn't sit up on this paspallium the way it does on Zoysiagrass. But fescue — now you're talkin' grass!

■ Never be a real test of golf until they get rid of that stupid tree on 13, that Mickey Mouse bunker on 16 and that ridiculous ocean on 18!

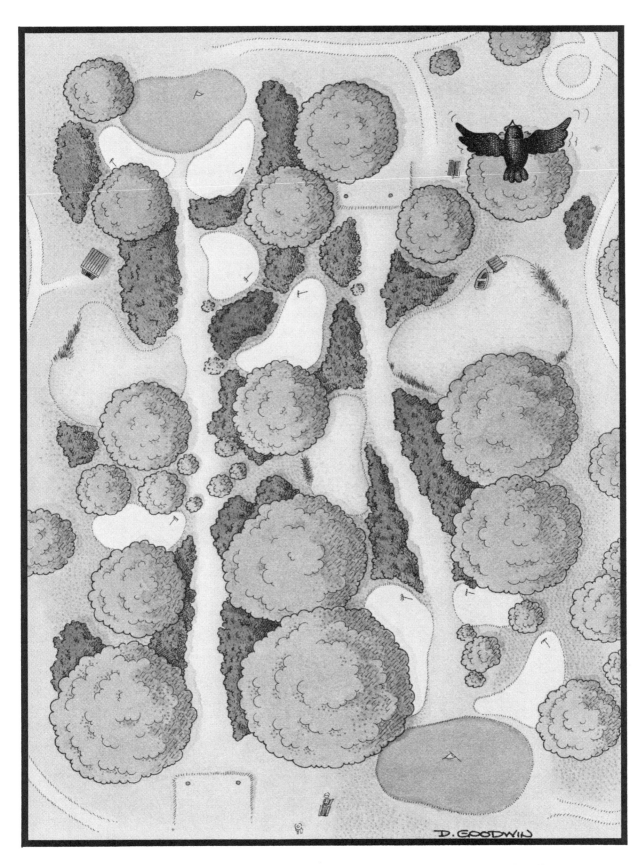

"Fairways are so tight its enough to make a bowler's butt pucker."

"I don't care what the pros say..."

- A tree is 90% tree!

- I don't mind keeping a course natural, but one cactus and a tumbling tumbleweed is not my idea of a port-a-john!

- That's the last time I trust sprinkler-head yardages written in Crayola.

- When you play a course they call *The Sistine Chapel* of golf, it's hard not to look up — a lot!

"I don't care what the pros say. A tree is 90% <u>tree</u>!"

The Great Architects

Golf course architects love to do it to us. They create holes that encourage one to believe in the miracle of making birdie, the hope of making par, the good sense to accept a bogey, and ultimately relieved to salvage no worse than a double bogey and the courage to stagger bravely to the next tee.

The very best of today's course designers understand that golfers are people who enjoy punishment. It is no accident they design courses or specific holes that cut right to the masochist in us — particularly those of us who have an ego only slightly bigger than our handicap.

As it was for the Marquis de Sade before, the theme song for today's successful golf designer is *Twist And Shout*.

"Tough? TOUGH??..."

- The only way you can survive the desert *waste areas* is to have a fore-caddie who looks like Gunga Din.

- There are so many logs and railroad ties shoring up tees and greens and bunkers and split fairways, the course is a damned fire hazard!

- They've got traps so deep you need a Sherpa caddie to help you climb out.

- The locals won't even tee it up until after four or five — stiff drinks!

- They made me sign my scorecard in blood — the little I had left!

"I'll say it's a killer course..."

- They always stick the ladies tees right in my line of flight!

- I even lost a ball in the ball washer!

- When you've got a 15-foot snake to save par, you better count the rattles before stroking it.

- I saw Sir Edmund Hillary out there and he had to walk <u>around</u> the greens!*

Well that's what Tom Weiskopf said and he got away with it.

"The ladies tees are a real killer..."

"Don't you hate these new courses where..."

- All the holes are surrounded by condos and everybody and his brother is always watching you!

- The green fees are so expensive you have to play every square yard and shoot 148 just to get your money's worth!

- They even have a dress code for the alligators. They make 'em wear embroidered little golfers on their chests.

"... all the holes are surrounded by condos
and everybody is always watching you."

2

Meteorlogical

It's always safe to blame the weather... almost always.

The fact is that there is no such thing as bad weather to a real golf lover.

Neither wind, nor rain, nor sleet, nor snow keep a real golfer from his appointed rounds.

But if Mother Nature does get a little too frightening, just remember the words of Lee Trevino who said: *When God wants to play through, you let him play through.*

Amen!

"When God wants to play through..."

Winter

- It was so cold, my orange balls turned purple — so did my other ones!

- There was some major moisture coming down — I swear I saw this big funny-looking boat with all these animals two-by-two floating past the driving range.

- It rained so hard even the ducks had umbrellas.

- Cold?? My Golden Bear headcovers went into hybernation and I couldn't get my driver out til Spring!

Spring

- I don't care what Mr. Groundhog says, it's not golf season until I can put a tee in the ground without the help of an ice pick.

- I know spring has sprung — but so has the IRS. Give me a break!

Summer

- *Summertime and the livin' is easy, fish are jumpin' —* How can you concentrate on golf with all those damn fish jumpin'?!

- It was so hot, my balls got a tan.

- It was really an oven out there — I needed two gloves and a potholder to get an iron out of my bag.

- It was so humid, by the time I was ready to swing I had sweated my ball into a water hazard.

- It was so hot, the white tee-markers looked like raisins.

Fall

- A little windy?? The course played so long it took a driver, two 3-woods, a 4-iron and a wedge just to get from my cart to the first tee!

- It was blowing dead in my face at the tee, dead downwind at the green, and inbetween was so tricky even the seagulls were walking!

- It was downwind all right. Hit an easy 9-iron and flew the green by 30 yards, but found my divot three feet from the hole!

- Blew so hard there were whitecaps in the port-a-johns.

- Club selection gets a little tough when it's coming at you hard enough to blow the freckles off your face.

- Look, guys from Texas and Florida are good wind players. I'm from California. We're good at buying Mercedes and ordering dinner at expensive restaurants.*

*Well, that's what Gary McCord said... Don't think he got away with it either.

"... just hard enough to blow the freckles off your face."

A SEPTEMBER SONG FOR GOLFERS

When Maxwell Anderson wrote, *Oh it's a long, long while from May to December...* he obviously wasn't speaking for golfers. It's never long enough to play the grand old game!

When the Autumn weather turns the leaves to flame...

Good luck finding your ball under all those flaming leaves. Sure, you'll find a dozen others — but not yours!

*One hasn't got time for
the waiting game.*

The only one who hasn't got time is the foursome behind waiting for you to find your ball!

*And the days dwindle down, to a
precious few, September, November...*

Which means no more daylight savings time! You're lucky if you can get in three holes after work.

*And these few precious days,
I'll spend with you. These precious days,
I'll spend with you...*

Can only mean curling up in front of the fireplace with the VCR and Bobby Jones,' *How I Play Golf* Volumn I and II.

YOUR GREATEST EXCUSES

Natural Forces:

■ _____
_____
_____

■ _____
_____
_____

■ _____
_____

■ _____
_____
_____

■ _____
_____
_____

■ _____
_____
_____

■ _____
_____
_____

■ _____
_____
_____

■ _____
_____
_____

■ _____
_____
_____

"Ahhh, ya should've been here last week, me boy — <u>before</u> they cut the rough!"

PART IV

INTERNATIONAL

Given the universal nature of the grand old game, most golf excuses apply to players from Greenland to Guam, Tunisia to Tobago and all points between. Probably because we all share the same humiliation and torture of body, mind and spirit, wherever we tee it up.

However, because of certain cultural, geographical and ideological differences of nations there are some excuses uniquely indigenous to specific countries — excuses which, in truth, are only meaningful and effective when used in their homeland.

It will be helpful to remember that when playing golf outside the United States most courses rely on more natural conditions and not artificial hazards to provide the challenge.

Here then are some of the best and most highly playable excuses from:

■ *Russia* ■ *Japan* ■ *France* ■ *Switzerland*
■ *Italy* ■ *Israel* ■ *Spain* ■ *Scotland*

Russia

- I know Comrade Gorbachev likes to call it Pebble Beach North, but it's still Siberia to me.

- The OB on 18 is no picnic, but it's the KGB at the 19th hole that's the real ball-breaker!

- What chance does a good Communist have when Glasnost entitles <u>everyone</u> to a Baryshnikov on the first tee!

"Glasnost entitles everyone to a Baryshnikov on the first tee."

Japan

■ Nobody plays in five hours! Need all day to enjoy train ride to course, traditional golf breakfast of raw egg, seaweed, soybean soup, dried fish, pickles and green tea, play nine holes, soak in hot bath, have blowfish sushi for snack, sip sake, warm up for back nine starting time, play golf, get back in hot bath, have few beers and catch train home. Now that golf!

■ Difficult to concentrate when all women caddies look like Flying Nun and say only two things: *Bunkahh* and *Iz O.B.*

■ When opponent in foursome yell *BONSAI!* he not about to attack, he describing tree you just hit ball into.

■ Can't afford to play anymore since unlucky hole-in-one last month. Had to spring for drinks for all people in club, give engraved silver pens to all best friends, give embroidered towels to not-so-best friends, donate tree to course and throw big humdinger party for all golfers and anybody else who hear about hole-in-one misfortune. Now mortgage house just to finance mid-week starting time on fourth floor of driving range!

"Now, that golf!"

France

- The sand traps I can handle, but the vineyards are hell to play out of!

- The guillotine-shaped scoreboard behind the 18th gives a whole new meaning to the word *choked*.

- When driving to golf in Paris, you must remember this, *a kiss is still a kiss, a sigh is just a sigh,* and the sidewalks, parking strips and center dividers are all in play!

- The front 9's are all crepe suzettes. It's the backside when the escargots catch up to you!

"... the vineyards are hell to play out of."

Switzerland

- It takes at least four lessons before you realize that when a Zurich pro is explaining *Swiss movement and perfect timing,* he's <u>not</u> talking about his golf swing!

- Golf in the Alps can give you a real natural high...

- We find it in our best interests to remain neutral when it comes to discussing Swiss golf excuses.

"... a real natural high!"

Italy

"When in Rome..."

■ Most of the rough is like playing out of pasta — in fact, it <u>is</u> pasta!

■ The greens are tempermental. Impossible to figure out. Some days everything breaks towards Vesuvius, some days toward the Vatican. Go figure?

"When in Sicily..."

■ If the local pros want to play through, you let them play through.

■ You make your bets on the first tee, your partners decide your handicap on the 18th, and make you an offer you can't refuse at the 19th hole.

■ It's not considered polite to ask a member of the Sicilian National Golf Club how many holes-in-one he's had.

"When the local pros want to play through..."

Israel

- You try playing golf when your caddie is your mother and she has all the answers — also all the questions!

- It isn't easy to lie about your handicap when the pro at your home course is also your Rabbi. Trust me.

- The course is for nebishes. It's the blintzes at the 19th hole deli you come to play. Such a game!

"You try playing when your caddie is your mother..."

Spain

- The courses are so tough you need 14 clubs and a cape.
- Before teeing off in Madrid you need a lesson from the local Matador.
- In Pamplona it's not the cow pies on the front side you have to worry about, it's the bull on the back you don't want to step into.
- In Seville all the caddies look like Sancho Panza — and all the holes look like *the impossible dream*.

*"In Pamplona it's not the cow pies on the front side
you have to worry about..."*

Scotland

- The birthplace of the grand old game where the gorse and the heather and the driving rain and freezing wind make a golfer need a 19th hole after every hole! Now, me boy, when the weather gets bad...

- When you're looking for your ball in the rough, never put your bag down — you may find your ball, but...

- When one of the old pros at the Loch Ness Links tells you to play it as it lies, laddie, you play it as it lies!

"When one of the old pros at the Loch Ness Links tells you to play it as it lies, laddie..."

"Reading about golf excuses is like going to see the doctor. You're not there to be told you're burning the candle at both ends. You came to get more wax!"

THE TRUTH YOU ALWAYS SUSPECTED...

When it comes to golf excuses, it's like Tina Turner says, *What's truth got to do with it — got to do with it...*

Yes, an excuse may actually have some semblance of truth to it, but so what?

We're talking about golf here! Far more important than the *truth* is what we <u>need</u> to believe about our own mastery of the game — or perhaps more correctly what we need others to believe.

How else can you explain why there are not only golfers who somehow always play a few strokes better than their card-carrying handicap suggests they should, but also golfers whose scores rarely live up to their single-digit handicap — golfers who need to think of themselves as really *players* in spite of a preponderance of evidence to the contrary. (It's what happens when one's ego refuses to accept one's handicap. And it can be hazardous to one's financial health. Trust me.)

And finally, if the truth were really good enough, we wouldn't need great excuses!

Besides, who are we kidding? We already know the truth: That, with fleeting exceptions, we will always play better in our minds and hearts than we do on the course; that we will never be as good as we think we are; and the day we achieve our greatest golfing fantasies is the day we'll probably quit. And of course, to a true golfer, that is unthinkable!

So, when all is said and putted out on 18, if the excuses you've reached for during the round aren't exactly something you'd want to swear to before Judge Wapner, don't feel too guilty.

Try to remember that, at various times, golf has been defined as:

■ *A game whose aim is to hit a very small ball into an even smaller hole with weapons singularly ill-designed for the purpose,* at least according to Sir Winston Churchill.

■ *A game where the ball invariably lies poorly and the golfer well!*

■ *A lot of walking broken up by disappointment and bad arithmatic.*

And it is indeed all of the above and more. Which is why we need all the great excuses we can get to keep swinging.

For come hell, high water, quadruple bogey or quadruple bypass, a golfer's gotta do what a golfer's gotta do to make it to that last roundup!

If your alibis give you the courage to play again, that's all that matters.

OTHER GOLF BOOKS BY MARK OMAN

**The 9 Commandments of Golf... According to The Pro Upstairs —
Cosmic Secrets for Mastering the Game!**
Illustrated by Doug Goodwin
(112 pages — 20 illustrations) ISBN 0-917346-07-6 $6.95

Discover the glory of golf, as it is in Heaven and ought to be on Earth!

*"A lot of God's ideas for Earth haven't always worked out. Take that
Moses thing... You haven't even gotten the 10 Commandments right yet!
God knows what you'll do with 9 Commandments just for golf... Actually,
even He doesn't know. But He's got to try something!!"*
The Pro Upstairs

**The Sensuous Golfer — How To Play The Game... On The Course And
Off!**
Illustrated by Tom Nix
(72 pages — 32 illustrations) ISBN 0-917346-01-7 $6.95

Whether you keep it in your bag or under your bed, this book will put
you in position to play around with the best of 'em!

*"The perfect gift for the passionate player who has all the equipment —
but doesn't know what to do with it!"*
Joan Rivers

**How To Live With A Golfaholic — A Survival Guide for Family and
Friends of Passionate Players**
Illustrated by Jay Campbell and Carl Christ
(96 pages — 20 illustrations) ISBN 0-917346-14-9 $6.95

The only book to help you survive the traps and hazards of a golfer's
magnificent obsession.

"Mark Oman's observations are all in the birdie circle."
Charles M. Schulz

Portrait Of A Golfaholic
Illustrated by Gary Patterson
(96 pages — 30 illustrations) ISBN 0-8092-5335-6 $6.95

The bible of Golfaholics Anonymous. A look into the wide world of
golfaholism.

*"A great gift to the guy in your foursome who is always pressing for
6 A.M. tee times... Every sinner loves company."*
Los Angeles Times